The Ever-Living Tree

The Life and Times of a Coast Redwood

Linda Vieira

Illustrations by
Christopher Canyon

Walker and Company
New York

First published in the United States of America in 1994 by Walker Publishing Company, Inc.; first paperback edition published in 1996.
Published simultaneously in Canada by Thomas Allen & Son Canada, Limited, Markham, Ontario

Library of Congress Cataloging-in-Publication Data
Vieira, Linda.
    The ever-living tree : the life and times of a coast redwood / by Linda Vieira ;
illustrations by Christopher Canyon.
      p. cm.
    ISBN 0-8027-8277-9.—ISBN 0-8027-8278-7 (lib bdg)
    1. Redwood—Juvenile literature. [1. Redwood.] 1. Canyon, Christopher, ill. II. Title.
QK494.5.T3V54 1994
584'.2—dc20
ISBN 0-8027-7477-6 (paper)

                                                                     93-31688
                                                                        CIP
                                                                         AC

Printed in Hong Kong

This book is dedicated to Debbie, Shelley, and Michael for inspiring me, and to my wonderful Nick for his love.

L. V.

To Jeanette, Dad, and Goppy.

C. C.

It was a cool, foggy morning in a forest near the ocean when the little tree first poked itself up out of the ground. There were other trees in the evergreen forest just like it. Some were taller, some fatter, some older.

Eventually scientists would call this tree *Sequoia sempervirens*, an *ever-living sequoia*. It would also be known as a *coast redwood*.

More than 50 million years before this tree began to grow, different kinds of redwood trees grew all over the world. They lived at the same time as the dinosaurs until the *glaciers* came. Those slow-moving rivers of ice made many plants and animals extinct.

MACEDONIA
THRACE
BLACK   SEA
RUSSIA
ASIA MINOR
CASPIAN
SEA
PUNJAB
MEDITERRANEAN
SEA
CYPRUS
BACTRIA
PARTHIA
PHOENICIA
EGYPT
PERSIAN GULF
GEDROSIA
RED SEA
INDIA
ALEXANDER'S
EMPIRE

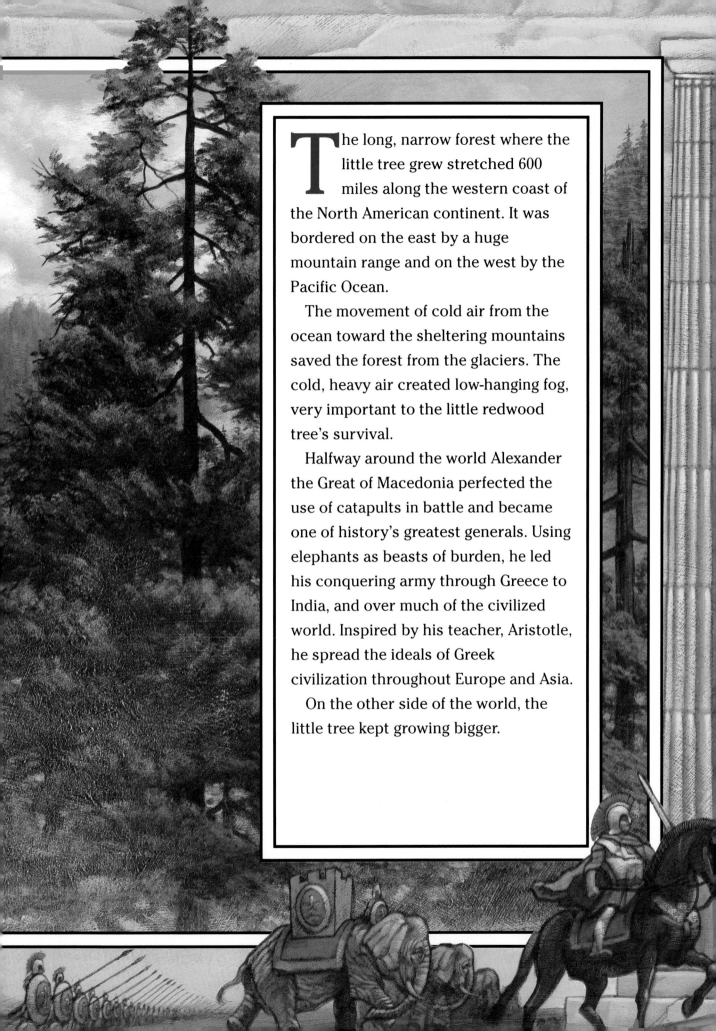

The long, narrow forest where the little tree grew stretched 600 miles along the western coast of the North American continent. It was bordered on the east by a huge mountain range and on the west by the Pacific Ocean.

The movement of cold air from the ocean toward the sheltering mountains saved the forest from the glaciers. The cold, heavy air created low-hanging fog, very important to the little redwood tree's survival.

Halfway around the world Alexander the Great of Macedonia perfected the use of catapults in battle and became one of history's greatest generals. Using elephants as beasts of burden, he led his conquering army through Greece to India, and over much of the civilized world. Inspired by his teacher, Aristotle, he spread the ideals of Greek civilization throughout Europe and Asia.

On the other side of the world, the little tree kept growing bigger.

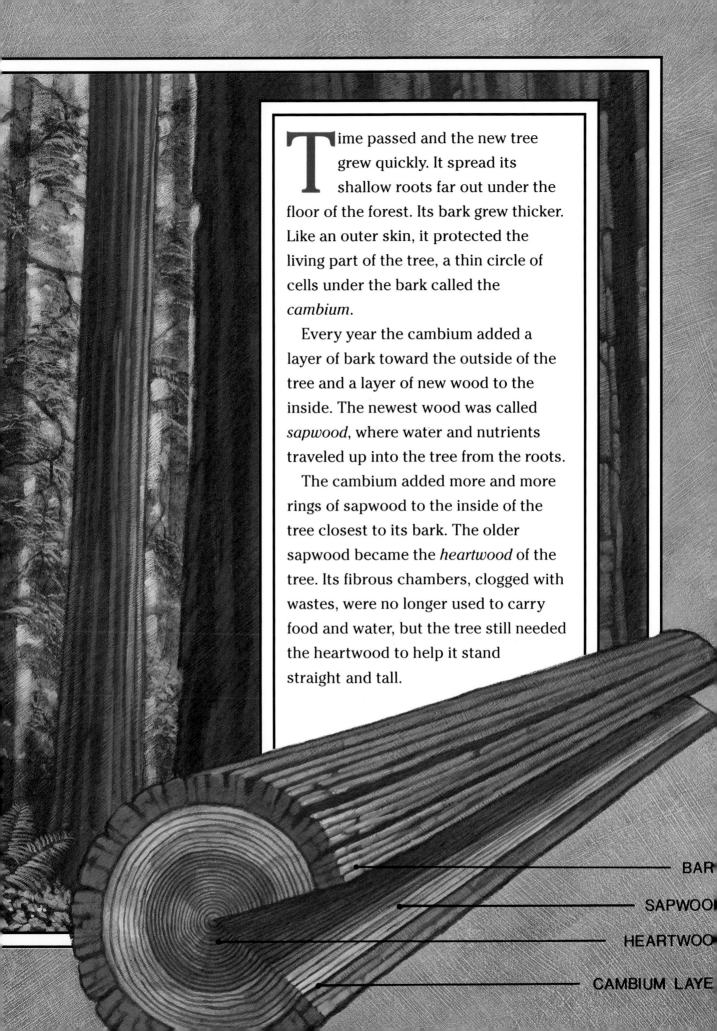

Time passed and the new tree grew quickly. It spread its shallow roots far out under the floor of the forest. Its bark grew thicker. Like an outer skin, it protected the living part of the tree, a thin circle of cells under the bark called the *cambium*.

Every year the cambium added a layer of bark toward the outside of the tree and a layer of new wood to the inside. The newest wood was called *sapwood*, where water and nutrients traveled up into the tree from the roots.

The cambium added more and more rings of sapwood to the inside of the tree closest to its bark. The older sapwood became the *heartwood* of the tree. Its fibrous chambers, clogged with wastes, were no longer used to carry food and water, but the tree still needed the heartwood to help it stand straight and tall.

BAR

SAPWOO

HEARTWOO

CAMBIUM LAYE

ime went on. Dozens of trapping spiders looked for spaces up and down the thick, uneven bark of the tree. They stretched their webs wherever they could. The outside of the tree looked like an apartment house for spiders. The webs didn't hurt the tree at all. It just kept growing.

Across the ocean in China, men began building a great stone wall along their borders for protection against their enemies. Built entirely by hand of earth, brick, and stone, it took millions of workers hundreds of years to complete. The Great Wall eventually stretched more than 1,500 miles across mountains and valleys.

Thousands of miles to the east, the little redwood tree grew and grew.

The cold morning air was heavy with moisture, but soon the sun found its way through the thick trees to the forest floor. The air became warmer and the moisture began to evaporate. The warmed air rose as it lost moisture and became lighter. The air currents gently pushed insects higher and higher. Some were trapped by the waiting webs along the bark.

A small group of native women came into the forest to collect acorns, pine nuts, ferns, and other plants beneath the tree. They belonged to a peaceful Native American tribe called *Ohlone*.

Although they gathered what they needed from the redwood forest, the natives did not live there. They considered the forest a sacred place, with its giant trees and ferocious grizzly bears. They did their gathering quickly and left, thanking the Great Spirit for such a bounty.

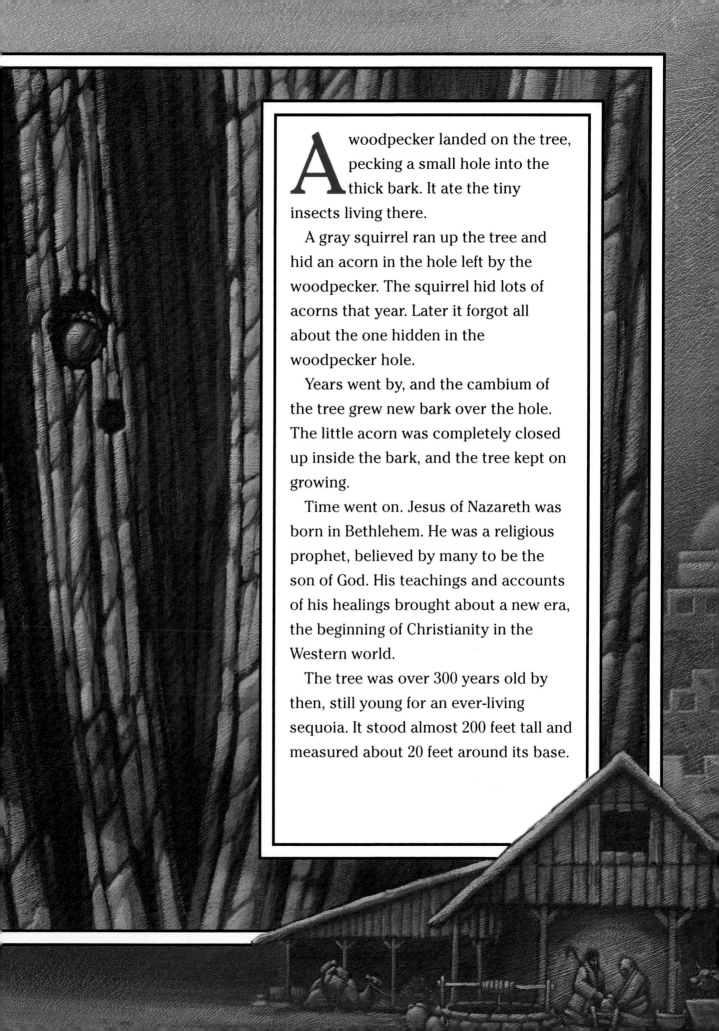

A woodpecker landed on the tree, pecking a small hole into the thick bark. It ate the tiny insects living there.

A gray squirrel ran up the tree and hid an acorn in the hole left by the woodpecker. The squirrel hid lots of acorns that year. Later it forgot all about the one hidden in the woodpecker hole.

Years went by, and the cambium of the tree grew new bark over the hole. The little acorn was completely closed up inside the bark, and the tree kept on growing.

Time went on. Jesus of Nazareth was born in Bethlehem. He was a religious prophet, believed by many to be the son of God. His teachings and accounts of his healings brought about a new era, the beginning of Christianity in the Western world.

The tree was over 300 years old by then, still young for an ever-living sequoia. It stood almost 200 feet tall and measured about 20 feet around its base.

One day there was a big fire in the forest and many trees burned. Flames ate into the redwood tree near the ground. Fire-resistant elements in the heartwood finally stopped the fire, leaving a low, hollowed-out cave inside.

The cambium of the tree was not hurt badly by the fire. It continued to grow new bark around the opening of the cave. Over many years, the new bark almost closed up the opening, while the inside stayed hollow. The tree grew on and on.

Almost nine thousand miles southeast of the forest lay the continent of Africa. In a grassy *savanna* at the edge of the vast Sahara desert, the kingdom of Kanem flourished as a major commercial center. Caravans brought metalware, horses, and salt from North Africa and Europe to trade there for ivory and kola nuts from the south.

In the peaceful forest far away to the west, the redwood tree stood tall and strong.

Tiny striped chipmunks ran up and down the tree. They nestled on a branch that grew in a strange and different way. The branch had become a *burl*. Its wood was curled into a lump cozy enough for a chipmunk to rest upon. The burl didn't stop the tree from growing higher and wider. By now it was over 250 feet tall. It was more than 50 feet around the bottom. It grew and grew and grew.

A trader named Marco Polo traveled with his father and uncle from Europe to China. They were the first outsiders ever to be welcomed in China. They found gold, jewels, silks, and spices never before seen by Europeans.

When they returned home, Marco Polo described the advanced customs they had found in China—a postal system, paper money, and the use of coal as fuel.

The redwood tree grew taller and thicker. Its new rings of wood grew closer together like pages of a book. Its bark was almost a foot thick. Its twisted roots sent *root crown sprouts* up through the ground, encircling the tree in a *fairy circle*.

Another, smaller fire swept through the forest, clearing away loose brush from around the tree. Dense fibers in the tree snuffed out the flames again before there was any damage.

BCE
325
356-323
305
214
155
CE
1
700

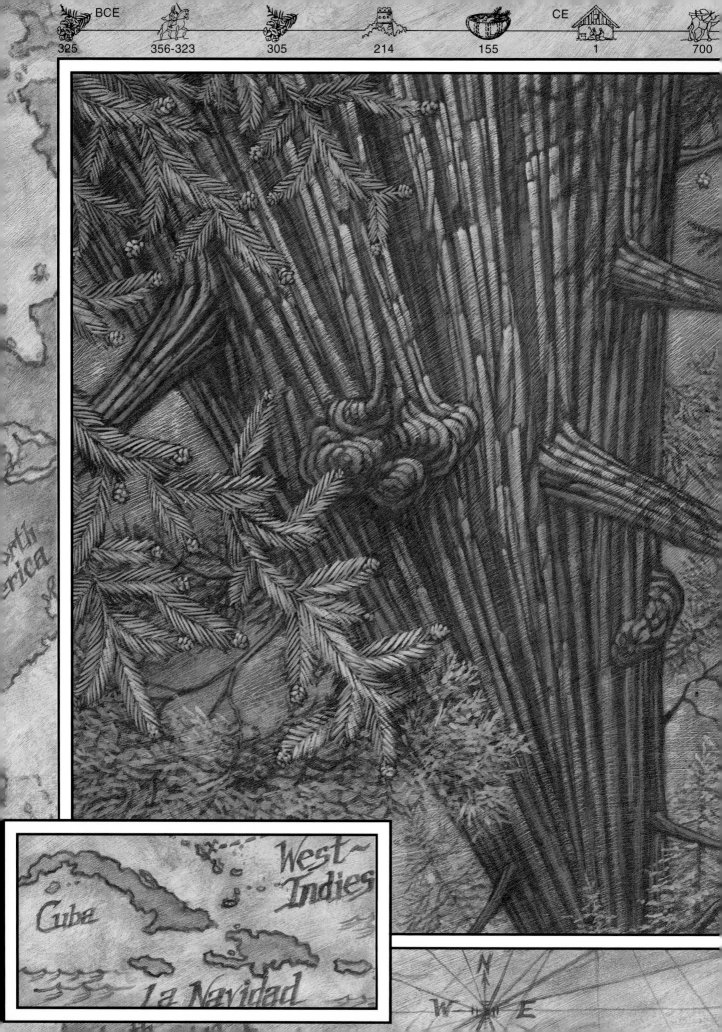

Cube

West~
Indies

La Navidad

North
America

N
W E

Redwood cones fell from the tree's high branches. Many burst open when they landed, and some of their tiny seeds sprouted into new trees.

An Italian explorer named Christopher Columbus wanted to find a new route to China. Inspired by the explorations of Marco Polo, he persuaded the queen of Spain to finance his voyage through uncharted seas to the west. Although Columbus did not reach China, he landed at the southeastern part of North America and called it the New World.

The redwood tree was almost 3,000 miles away from where Columbus landed, still growing in its sheltered forest far to the west.

BCE 325 356-323 305 214 155 CE 1 700

Deer walked the trails of the forest and found hidden areas to protect them from their enemies while they grazed on the lush vegetation.

Gray foxes lived in the forest, too. Some of their babies were born inside the tree's sheltered cave.

Birds nested in the topmost branches of the tallest, oldest trees. Mammals, birds, insects, and reptiles lived together, replenishing their species every year according to a natural balance.

On the northeastern coast of North America, a small ship called the *Mayflower* brought a group of pilgrims to the New World. Many of them had been oppressed, and dreamed of a land where freedom of religion would prevail. The pilgrims struggled to live through their first terrible winter in the New World.

On the opposite coast, the tree provided a home for a mother raccoon and her babies. The cave kept them warm and dry, safe from the grizzly bears and mountain lions.

Time went on and on. The ever-living redwood tree kept growing bigger and bigger. It stood tall and silent in the middle of its fairy circle of younger trees.

The United States of America declared itself an independent nation in the New World with thirteen colonies along the eastern coast of North America. General George Washington led the colonists through the bitter Revolutionary War with Great Britain to establish that independence. After the war, General Washington became the first president of the United States.

The giant redwood tree was now more than 300 feet tall—one of the tallest living things on the face of the earth.

One day there was a terrible storm in the forest. Wind and rain lashed at the trees. Claps of thunder made the animals run and hide. A flashing bolt of lightning struck the base of the tree at its weakest part, near the cave. The tree fell over on its side with a tremendous crash. Its huge trunk broke into pieces when it hit the ground.

Gold was discovered in the western territories of North America. Thousands of people crossed the continent in horse-drawn wagons, dreaming of riches and new opportunities.

Boom towns and cities grew quickly. Hunters, loggers, tanners, and miners exploited the resources of the land. Soon a railroad reached across the continent from coast to coast. Trains carried settlers to places near the redwood forest, where the vigorous roots of the fallen tree kept growing.

Time went on. The life force of the ever-living sequoia would not die. Its roots gave life and strength to the smaller trees around it. Soon a new tree began to grow up from the broken trunk.

Millions of insects used the bark of the old tree for food. Over many years the wood began to change into a fine dust. Banana slugs changed the dust into *organic elements*, which went back into the soil as nutrients.

In outer space, a man walked on the moon for the first time. People watched him on television screens all over the world. Astronauts and cosmonauts from different countries traveled into space. Scientists planned to build a space station hundreds of miles from Earth.

Today people camp in the shelter of the tree, and children play games on its decomposing log. They are amazed at its length—longer than a football field.

In the narrow, ancient forest, the ever-living sequoias keep growing. They stand like giant statues as millions of visitors from all over the world come to marvel at their incredible height.

Tiny new trees poke themselves up out of the ground. Life in a coast redwood forest goes on and on.